DON'T WRECK YOUR SOCIAL SECURITY DISABILITY CLAIM

Law Offices of Lisa Douglas
2300 Main Street
North Little Rock, AR 72114
501-798-0004

739 South 7th Street
Suite 2
Heber Springs, AR 72543
www.LisaGDouglas.com

------------------Law Offices of Lisa Douglas, PLLC----------

DISCLAIMER

This Book is Not Legal Advice

This information is general in nature and should not be relied on as a substitute for legal advice.

This book is provided as an education service by Law Offices of Lisa Douglas.

TABLE OF CONTENTS

FOREWORD

If you can answer YES to the following questions, I may be the lawyer for you.

1. Are you no longer able to work 8 hours a day, 5 days a week, due to your disability?

2. Is your medical condition disabling?

3. Are you unable to perform the work that you previously did?

4. Are you unable to perform any other job?

5. Have you received the treatment your medical doctor prescribed and followed your medical doctor's recommendations?

If you can answer YES to each of these questions, give Lisa Douglas a call at 501-798-0004

WHY THIS BOOK?

I wrote this book because, if you are like most, this is the first time you have applied for Social Security Disability and you have many questions. Many times I have found the questions come too late and, as a result, the disabled person pays because his or her lack of information. Educating yourself about the application process is the first step to improving your success.

It is not uncommon for a disability claim to initially be denied. Research shows that over 75% of those who initially apply for benefits are denied. However, research also shows that more than 75% of persons who appeal their cases and have legal representation are later approved for benefits.

As a disabled person, no one needs to remind you how difficult life has been. When you have your health you take it for granted. But when you become disabled, your life turns upside down. When you were working, life was great and you were productive.

This book was written to help guide you through this difficult period of time in your life. In many cases it will take approximately two years be-fore your claim is actually decided.

If you have not already received "*Documenting Disability for Health Care Providers,*" request a copy by calling or e-mailing my office. This companion book is designed to guide your health care providers in their documentation of your disability according to the guidelines as set out by the Social Security Ad-ministration.

I wrote this book for **you.** Hopefully you will find it will give you some valuable information to consider on your own time.

This book is too limited to explore every issue or address each possible question you may have.

Further, this book is not intended to give legal advice and nothing in this book is legal advice. Obtaining this book from me does not create an attorney-client relationship between us. I do not sign up everyone who calls my office.

Determination of Disability

The Social Security Administration has developed a five step test to determine if you are disabled according to their definition. When a claim is initially filed, it will go through this five step evaluation process.

The five questions to consider in determining whether or not you are disabled according to the strict definition as set out by the Social Security Administration are as follows:

1.   Are you gainfully employed? Gainfully employed means you make more than $940.00 per month or more.

2.   Is your condition severe? (The condition can be mental or physical or both, either way it interferes with your basic activities at work.)

3.   Is your condition found in their list of disabling conditions?   (You can find these online through the SSA website at: *www.socialsecurity.gov/ disability/professionals/bluebook/AdultListings.htm*

4.   Can you do the work you previously did?

5.   Can you do any other type of work?

These factors are a checklist to determine your potential eligibility for Social Security Disability benefits. If you are not working, then you proceed to step two to determine if your condition interferes with work related activities. If it does not then you are not considered disabled. So, overall, you must pass the first two criteria before your claim will be considered.

If you are not gainfully employed and your condition does interfere with work then you proceed to step three. Under step three if your condition is found in their list of medical conditions then you are automatically deemed disabled. If your condition is not found on their list of medical conditions then you proceed to step four.

Here at step four, they must determine if your medical condition interferes with your ability to perform the work you previously did. If it does then you proceed to step five. If you cannot perform your previous job, is there any other job you can perform? Here they consider your age, education, work experience, and any skills you may have. If you cannot adjust to other work, your claim will be approved. However, if you can adjust to other work, your claim will be denied.

Remember if your job is becoming more and more difficult to perform, due to the disability, this is irrelevant.

In summary there are two ways to be found disabled under this Social Security Administration checklist: (1) A finding that the claimant's impairment meets an impairment described in their listing of impairments; or (2) A combination of the medical and vocational issues qualifies the claimant for disability.

Do I Need An Attorney?

You do not have to retain an attorney. Legal representation is not required for any portion of the Social Security Disability application process or the appeal to the Administrative Law Judge (ALJ). However, retaining an attorney at the beginning of your claims process could increase your chances of prevailing at the beginning of the process.

How Do I Afford An Attorney?

The attorney only receives a fee if they win your case. So they are paid only after they win your case. This fee is paid out of your potential back benefits. An attorney can only receive 25% of your back benefits up to a maximum amount after they have won your case.

Your attorney can charge for out of pocket expenses, which are separate and apart from the attorney's fee. Out of pocket expenses would include expenses such as paying for your medical records from your doctor. You should speak to your attorney beforehand to determine if you will be responsible for paying for these out of pocket expenses.

The Application

The first step is the application process. You can submit your application by mail, phone or online If you complete your application by mail or online, you should always fill out the application completely. It is the claimant's responsibility to make sure the application is accurate and completely filled out. Be sure to answer every question on the application. If you do not understand the question, call your local Social Security Office and ask for help.

Be sure you list every one of your illness, whether or not you think it contributes to your inability to work. There may be instances where the symptoms of different illnesses may collectively contribute to an inability to work, that perhaps you were unaware of.

List every one of your treating physicians (including mental health care providers), clinics or hospitals. This will provide a progressive view of your illnesses. If there is not enough room on the application to list these, attach an additional sheet.

In the work section give complete answers to the questions. This section refers to what you used to do, not what you are able to do now.

Be sure and make copies of everything you send to the Social Security Disability Administration. If you move or your phone number changes, make sure you have provided this new information to them.

Determination of Disability

Your medical records are the heart of your case. The Social Security Disability Administration will request your medical records from the providers you listed on your application. That is why it is important to provide a complete list of your medical care providers. If you have been seen by additional health care providers or your illness has worsened, make sure you provide this new information. These records will help paint the picture of your current health status and, therefore, your capacity for work

The more medical documentation you have, the easier it will be to support your proof of disability.

Your medical records are the most important evidence in your file. If your medical records are insufficient, you may be required to see a medical doctor for a medical examination. This is provided for by the Social Security Administration at no cost to you.

Disability Defined

To qualify for social security disability, you must meet a strict criteria. Part of Social Security's definition of disability is the inability to work any job. That means that if you are a roofer and can no longer perform this strenuous job due to back problems, but you can sit and perform a less strenuous job like assembling watches on an assembly line, then you are not disabled under Social Security Administration's guidelines. Even working part time shows that you have the ability to work.

In addition the disability must be expected to last for twelve continuous months or be expected to end in death.

Further the condition must be a "medically determinable impairment." You cannot be determined to be disabled just because you say you are disabled. You have to have medical documentation to prove your disability. Your doctor must back up his/her medical diagnosis of your impairment with   medical history, diagnostic tests and laboratory results. (Get my book *Documenting Disability for Health Care Providers.*)

To summarize, in order to be found disabled for purposes of the social security administration your condition must be:
1.   A medically determinable impairment.
2.   Functionally limiting so that all work is precluded.
3.   Expected to last for twelve continuous months or be expected to end in death.

Don't let the Social Security Administration's definition of disability deter you from applying if you are unable to work.   If you are denied, they are required to provide you with a written explanation and then you can decide whether or not to appeal their decision.

Disabling Conditions

The listing of impairments (found at: *www.socialsecurity.gov/disability/professionals/bluebook/AdultListings.htm*) describes impairments that are considered severe enough to prevent someone from engaging in gainful employment. This listing is broken down into major body systems and are as follows:

1.00 Musculoskeletal System
2.00 Special Senses and Speech
3.00 Respiratory System
4.00 Cardiovascular System
5.00 Digestive System
6.00 Genitourinary Disorders
7.00 Hematological Disorders
8.00 Skin Disorders
9.00 Endocrine System
10.00 Impairments that Affect Multiple Body Systems
11.00 Neurological
12.00 Mental Disorders
13.00 Malignant Neoplastic Diseases
14.00 Immune System

As previously discussed, you can find these at the Social Security web site *www.ssa.gov* or you can order their free publication by calling 1-800-772-1213.

A favorable decision would require your medical condition meet one or more of these disabling conditions. This medical condition should be documented in your medical records with the diagnostic tests to prove this condition exists.

My Past Relevant Work?

When the Social Security Administration reviews your past relevant work, it considers how you performed that job. So if you were able to perform that job sitting or standing, but now you can no longer stand for very long periods of time you could be deemed able to return to work.

If you can still perform the easiest job that you once performed, then you are not considered disabled.

Your educational level is an important factor used by the Social Security Administration to determine disability as well. According to the Social Security Administration, the higher your level of education the easier it will be for you to perform some type of work.

Application Period

It takes approximately four to six months for your initial Social Security Disability Application to be processed. Some of that delay is due to the amount of time it takes to receive your medical records from the various providers.

During this application period, it is important that you keep the Social Security Administration informed of any changes in your address or phone number. If you move you should always make sure they know of your new address. Likewise if your phone number changes, you should make sure they know of your new phone number as well.

Appeals Process: Request For Reconsideration

If you are denied Social Security Disability at the application level, then in most states to appeal a denied application you fill out a form entitled "Request for Reconsideration." Essentially this involves a review of the records that are already in your file and you are given the opportunity to submit any new information if it exists. Without more, you are basically asking for this agency to go back and admit it was wrong in their initial denial of your disability benefits. The likelihood of prevailing on this review alone is slim, unless you have additional information that was not a part of your file. If you are still denied Social Security Disability benefits at this level then you proceed to appeal that decision and request a hearing before the ALJ.

Appeals Process: Request for a Hearing Before the Administrative Law Judge (ALJ)

The appeals process to request a hearing is so back logged that it takes approximately eighteen months or more for a hearing to be scheduled before the ALJ. When you receive your hearing letter it will advise you of the date and time of your hearing.

Accompanying this letter will be an acknowledgment that you must complete and return to the ALJ. This is to confirm you are aware of the date and time that has been set for your hearing and that you will be there. If you are unable to make this scheduled date, it is important that you contact the court immediately to arrange for a different date.

Before this hearing date, it is important that you review the documents contained in your file. Currently, Arkansas sends out a compact disc (CD) with copies of these documents that are contained within your file. It is important for you and your attorney to review the contents of this file to ensure all the records from your health care providers have been received. If any are missing it is important that you obtain these and submit them for inclusion into your file before the hearing. In addition if you have received treatment or additional diagnostic tests since you applied for SSDI, then it is also important that you gather these documents and submit them to be included within your file before the hearing.

Updating your file ensures that the ALJ has the most current information before deciding your claim.

Vocational Experts

A vocational expert is usually present at the hearing. A vocational expert will explain to the judge what type of work you performed and explain what type of skill level was involved with your past job, whether skilled, semi-skilled, or unskilled. The vocational expert will also explain what type of exertional level was called for in your past job, such as sedentary/sit down, light, medium or heavy. The ALJ needs this information to determine if your impairment would prevent you from returning to your past work. The vocational expert will assist the ALJ in making a determination whether you have acquired any skills that could transfer to a less demanding job.

Medical Experts

Somewhere within the body of the letter that you receive from the ALJ informing you of your hearing, it may state that a medical expert is scheduled to appear at your hearing. The fact that an expert has been scheduled should not be viewed negatively. Often the scheduling of experts is merely the personal preference of the ALJ.

The medical expert can also help explain the medical records. In doing so this expert may ask you additional questions regarding your medical condition and then offer an opinion to the ALJ based on your answers.

Fatal Mistakes That Could Destroy Your Social Security Disability Claim

✓ *Mistake #1: Ignore Deadlines.* Many, who are applying for Social Security Disability are so ill they have a difficult time keeping up with the deadlines imposed by the Social Security Administration. But the Social Security Administration has very strict deadlines which you cannot just ignore. If you receive a denial letter, you have only 60 days to appeal.

✓ *Mistake #2: Stopping Medical Treatment.* It is a commonly held belief that if a person stops receiving medical treatment for his/her condition, then they are no longer ill, but now they have recovered from this debilitating disease or condition. If there are significant gaps in treatment, this suggests you are not suffering from a disability; otherwise, you would be maintaining your treatment and care for whatever you suffer from that prevents you from being able to work. Remember your medical records are the heart of your case. They prove the severity of your condition. Without the support of your medical records, you have very little chance to win your case. Remember, it is difficult for an

ALJ or anyone else for that matter to give credence to your complaints or ailments if you have not continued to see a doctor for them. So if you are complaining of chronic pain it is important that you have ongoing documentation of treatment for this persistent chronic condition, such as treatment by a pain management doctor.

People who are applying for Social Security Disability often do not have the insurance or the funds to pay for treatment. But the treatment records, *i.e.* your medical records are the evidence that is relied on to prove the severity of your condition. Most claims do not contain enough medical documentation to win benefits.

There are programs in the community that you could qualify for in order to receive medical treatment. You should check with the local non profit facilities to see if they provide programs that you may qualify for. Your attorney could assist you in locating these resources.

✓ *Mistake #3: Relying on the consultative examiner to prove your disability claim.* The Social Security Administration may schedule you for an appointment with a "consultative examiner." Generally this consultative examiner (CE) is a medical doctor or psychologist specializing in the field of your disability. It is a mistake to merely rely on the CE's report to prove your disability claim. For this examining doctor does not know you as well as your treating doctor would. This examining doctor's report is limited to his/ her examination of you along with a review of your medical history and any diagnostic tests that may have been received to write a comprehensive report. This evaluation is limited as compared to an on going progress report provided by your treating doctor. In addition, remember the CE does not work for you, this doctor is paid by the Social Security Administration to obtain medical evidence and write a report.

✓ *Mistake #4: Ignoring Mail From the Social Security Administration.* Sticking your head in the sand does not benefit your situation. Although you may be feeling ill, tired or just do not want to deal with potentially bad news from the Social Security Administration, this is no time to ignore their correspondence. If the Social Security Administration sends you a letter requesting additional information or scheduled you for a consultative examination and you do not reply, you end up delaying your claim or worse yet risk having your claim denied.

✓ *Mistake #5: Failing to Keep Copies of Your Correspondence.* Sometimes forms or letters are misplaced at the Social Security Administration office. Protect yourself by making copies of anything you send to them.

✓ *Mistake #6: Delay Applying for Benefits.* Sometimes people delay applying for disability because they feel their condition will improve. In the interim, most have become unable to work and even end up quitting their job due to their inability to perform it. You should apply for Social Security Disability as soon as you and your medical doctor decide that your condition will prevent you from returning to work. Waiting to file could cost you benefits that you might not be able to recover. You should apply as soon as you stop working due to your disability, you do not have to wait for one year to apply.

Remember for approval, the Social Security Administration law requires one of the following: (1) you have already been disabled and out of work for one year, or (2) your doctors expect that you will be unable to work for a minimum of one year from the date you last worked, or (3) your medical condition is expected to result in death. **You do not have to be unemployed for one year before applying for Social Security Disability. If you have been told this, that information is incorrect.**

✓ *Mistake #7: Continue Working While Applying for Social Security Disability.* If you are capable of working you are not disabled. It is not enough to just show you are unable to return to the type of work you used to do. You also must be incapable of performing any other job. This claim should be backed up by your treating physician.

Four Deadly Sins That Can Wreck A
Social Security Disability Case

1. *Giving up.*

This could be the kiss of death to a claim. The application process can be very discouraging. However, if you are disabled and unable to work, you should not give up by failing to appeal your case to the ALJ. At least, at this level, you are able to explain in your own words to the judge why you have been unable to work.

2. *Failing to Meet Deadlines*

Remember, you only have 60 days to appeal. If you miss this deadline, you will have to start the application process all over again. This could cost you benefits.

3. *Going Into the Process Uneducated*

Some people believe the Social Security Disability claims process is just a matter of filling out a few forms and then waiting for the checks to come in. Since the Social Security Administration denies approximately 75% of first time claims, it is to your advantage that you become educated about the process. You need to understand what information the Social Security Administration is looking for so that you can build a strong case from the very beginning.

4.   *Under Representing Your Activity Level to SSA*

Some have lived with their disability for so long that this way of life has become normal to them. Therefore, when they attempt to explain their condition, they minimize the restrictions and difficulties they are experiencing due to their condition.

A Note From the Author

After reading this book, I hope you have more insight about the social security disability claims process than when you initially requested this book and began your investigation. This book will give you a headstart and get you thinking about the things that can affect your claim. My purpose in writing this book was to equip you with general information about how social security disability cases work and provide you with some things you should know to increase the chances of winning yours. After all, knowledge is power.

Please understand that I do not accept every case about which I am contacted. I carefully select the few cases that I will accept at any one time.